All About Trees

An illustrated guide to nature's giants

ARCTURUS

ARCTURUS

This edition published in 2022 by Arcturus Publishing Limited
26/27 Bickels Yard, 151–153 Bermondsey Street,
London SE1 3HA

Author: Polly Cheeseman
Illustrator: Iris Deppe
Designer: Stefan Holliland
Editor: Violet Peto
Consultant: Anne Rooney
Managing Editor: Joe Harris

ISBN: 978-1-3988-1118-8
CH010039NT
Supplier 29, Date 0622, PI 00002182

Printed in China

Contents

Tremendous Trees

Every animal on Earth needs trees ... and that includes you! Trees give us an important gas called **oxygen**. All animals and people need to breathe oxygen in order to live.

Trees provide homes and shelter for millions of different plants and animals. Wood from trees can be used to make buildings, furniture, and paper.

Trees produce food for animals and people, such as **seeds**, nuts, and fruit. Some creatures, such as insects, feed on the bark and leaves of trees.

Burning fossil fuels produces gases such as **carbon dioxide**. Trees convert this gas into oxygen. Too much carbon dioxide makes the world hotter, so trees help keep our planet a comfortable temperature for everything that lives here.

Large areas filled with trees are called forests and woodlands. They are important **habitats** (homes) for many different kinds of plants and animals.

Broadleaf Trees

There are lots of different types of trees. Broadleaf trees have lots of leaves that they lose in winter. They are also called **deciduous** trees. Deciduous trees grow in many parts of the world.

A broadleaf tree has leaves that are wide and flat in shape. Oak, maple, and beech are common types of broadleaf trees.

Horse chestnut leaf

Crown

The very top of a tree is called the crown. A broadleaf tree usually has a wide, bushy crown. Each type of tree has its own shape.

The branches of a broadleaf tree grow outward, away from the trunk. Its branches are often crooked. As it grows, the tree gets wider and taller.

Horse chestnut tree

Broadleaf trees grow flowers called blossoms. The flowers produce fruits and **seeds**. Birds and animals like to eat the seeds and fruit.

Blossoms

7

Wonderful Woodland

A woodland **habitat** is green and shady. In a **deciduous** woodland, the trees, plants, and even some animals change along with the seasons. Lots of plants and animals live among the trees.

Birch

Hazel

Woodpecker

Many woodland animals feed on the nuts, **seeds**, and berries from the trees. Some woodland creatures hibernate (sleep) during the cold winter months.

Sycamore

Oak

Bluebells

The trees give shelter and protection to many different plants and animals. Squirrels will scurry up a tree trunk to escape danger.

Plants that live here are able to live in the cool shade of the wood. In spring, a beautiful carpet of bluebells can be seen in some woodlands.

9

The Life of a Tree

Some trees can live for thousands of years. But even the oldest trees started as a small **seed**. Trees need warmth and light from the sun, and water from rain, to grow strong and healthy.

2

The seed sprouts a shoot, which pushes up through the surface of the soil. The tiny shoot is called a seedling.

1

Root

This seed is an acorn. It falls from the tree as the weather gets colder. Then, in the spring, the first root breaks through the outer layer of the acorn. This is called **germination**.

As the seedling grows taller and stronger, it begins to look like a small tree.

3

4

After many years, the tree becomes a "mature" oak tree. It can now flower and make acorns of its own.

5

Beetle

Fungus

An oak tree can live for hundreds of years. When it dies and rots, it becomes an important **habitat** and source of food for wildlife.

Lovely Leaves

A tree's leaves do an important job. They make food for the tree using sunlight, water, and air. This process is called photosynthesis.

Carbon dioxide from the air goes in through tiny holes in the underside of the leaf.

Stem

The tree's roots take in water from the ground. The water travels to the leaf through the stem and veins.

Leaves take in energy from the sunlight. The leaves are flat and wide to take in as much sunlight as they can.

Vein

The leaves turn the carbon dioxide and water into **oxygen** and a type of sugar called **glucose**.

The tree uses the glucose to grow. The veins carry glucose to rest of the tree. The leaves release oxygen into the air.

Leaf Rubbing

Leaves come in all shapes and sizes. Next time you go for a walk outdoors, collect some different types of leaves. Then use them to create a beautiful artwork!

Place your leaves on a sheet of paper. Arrange them however you like. You could create a scene or make a pattern.

A "simple leaf" has one segment, or blade, which is attached to a stem.

Beech

Cover the leaves with another piece of paper the same size. Holding the paper in place, carefully rub over each leaf with a crayon.

Keep rubbing over each leaf until your picture is finished. You don't need to stick to green crayons—try using blue, purple, or even create rainbow stripes!

A "compound leaf" is made up of lots of leaf-shaped leaflets connected to a stemlike middle part.

Can you spot the veins and stem in your leaf rubbings?

Are your leaves simple or compound?

Black walnut

Animal Homes

Many different creatures build their homes in and around trees. The trees can be a safe place to hide from predators. Trees also provide strong and sturdy building materials.

Beavers live in rivers near woodland. They cut down trees with their powerful teeth, and use the wood to build dams. The dams make pools where the beavers build their homes, called "lodges."

Drey

Lodge

Squirrels build nests called dreys in the hollows and branches of trees. They build a drey using twigs and leaves, then line it with moss and feathers to make it snug.

Hornets are a large type of wasp. Hornets live in groups called colonies. Their paper-like nests can be found in hollow trees. Hornet nests are made from chewed-up wood.

Tawny owls make their nests in holes in **deciduous** trees, such as oaks. They sleep during the day. At night, tawny owls hunt for mice and voles.

Dam

Amazing Rain Forest

A rain forest is warm and wet all year round. The Amazon Rain Forest in South America is the largest rain forest in the world. A rain forest has different "layers," where many types of plants and animals live.

The top of the trees is called the canopy. Monkeys swing from branch to branch, while bright birds fly through the canopy.

Cacao tree

Rubber tree

The bottom part of the rain forest is the forest floor. There isn't much sunlight, so not many plants grow here. Creatures feed on leaves that have fallen from above.

18

Only the tallest trees, such as Brazil-nut trees, grow through the top of the canopy. This part of the forest is called the "emergent layer."

The "undergrowth" is the layer below the canopy. Bushes and smaller trees grow here. Many trees have enormous leaves, so they can catch as much sunlight as possible.

Brazil-nut tree

Palm tree

Leafcutter ants

Strong and Sturdy

As a tree grows, it gets taller and wider. It produces new branches, which give the tree its shape. The thick trunk and tough bark give a tree its strength.

The bark is like the tree's skin. It helps to protect the tree from damage by animals. It also stops it from being harmed by very hot or cold weather.

Rings

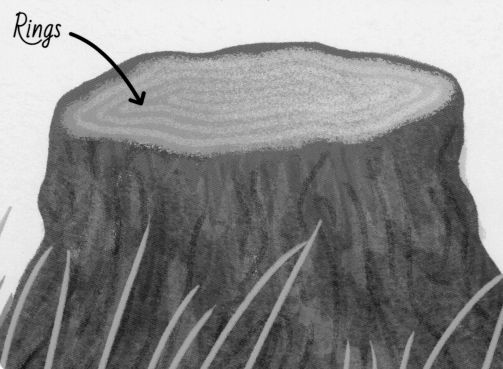

The tree trunk makes a new ring each year, as it grows upward and outward. You can tell how old a tree is by counting the rings.

Smooth bark

The bark near the base of the tree can be cracked and rough. As you look further up the tree, the bark gets smoother.

Rough bark

The trunk is wider at the base. The trunk is strong so that it can support the branches above. The distance around the trunk is called the girth.

Four Seasons

Broadleaf trees can look very different, depending on the time of year. Follow this red maple tree as it changes from season to season.

1

In spring, buds appear on the bare branches. As the days become longer and warmer, tiny flowers grow on the tree and green leaves grow.

Flowers

4

The leaves fall from the red maple tree. During the cold winter months, the branches stay bare—ready for it to begin all over again!

2

During the warm summer months, the tree is covered thickly with glossy, green leaves. The tree produces a "winged" fruit, which contains **seeds**.

Seeds

3

As the weather gets colder and there is less sunlight, the leaves start to change. They turn yellow, then orange, and finally bright red.

Making Seeds

New plants and trees grow from **seeds**. To make seeds, a plant needs **pollen** from another plant of the same type. This means pollen needs to move around.

Pollen

Many plants and trees use animals to spread their pollen. When bees collect **nectar** from a flower, they get covered in sticky pollen, which they then carry to other flowers.

When the plant has what it needs, it makes seeds. When the seeds have grown, they need to move to where they can grow. Many trees grow fruit around their seeds. The seeds are planted when an animal eats a piece of fruit and then poops out the seeds!

Spiky seeds called burrs can hitch a ride to a new spot by sticking to the fur of a passing animal.

Burrs

Some seeds float in the air. Next time you see a dandelion plant, blow on it and watch the seeds fly away.

25

Evergreen Trees

We call some trees "evergreen" because they stay green all year round. Unlike **broadleaf** trees, evergreens do not lose their leaves in winter. Evergreen trees can be found all over the world.

Evergreen leaves have a tough, waxy surface, which helps them hold onto water. The leaves can be shaped like needles, or like scales.

Douglas fir tree needle

Cone

Conifers are a type of evergreen tree. They do not have flowers or fruit. Instead, they produce cones which carry the tree's **seeds**. The cones have a scaly surface.

Conifers have tall, straight trunks, with regularly spaced branches. A conifer has an even shape, looking the same on both sides.

The wood from evergreen trees is very strong and is often used for buildings and furniture. Some conifers, such as pine and cypress trees, have a nice smell.

27

Coniferous Forest

A coniferous forest is a place that is filled with conifers. Coniferous forests are often found in cooler parts of the world.

Many conifers have special features to help them live in the cold. They have long, sharp needles. The needles allow snow to slide off them easily.

Pine

Nuthatch

Moose

Fir

Spruce

The trees of a coniferous forest include pines, firs, and spruces. They grow tall and straight and have a similar shape to each other.

Wolf

The animals that live in coniferous forests also have clever ways to cope with cold weather. Wolves have thick fur to keep them warm.

29

Beautiful Blossoms

Some trees put on a beautiful show in the springtime. Their branches are covered with pretty, sweet-smelling flowers called blossoms.

Japanese cherry blossom trees produce bright pink flowers. The blossoms usually only last for around a week before the petals float to the ground.

Inside each flower is a kind of sweet juice called **nectar** and a sticky powder called **pollen**. In order for the tree to make **seeds**, pollen needs to be spread to other trees.

The blossoms smell nice in order to attract insects, such as bees and butterflies. These creatures drink the nectar from the flowers and collect pollen on their bodies.

Once the blossoms on the tree have died away, the tree will go on to make fruit and seeds.

Extreme Trees

The tallest trees on Earth are Californian redwoods. These evergreen trees grow along the West Coast of the United States.

Redwoods can grow more than 100 m (330 ft) tall—that's taller than the Statue of Liberty! The base of the trunks can be 9 m (30 ft) wide.

They have somewhat shallow roots compared to their great height. This means that the trees sway in the wind. Occasionally, they fall over.

It takes hundreds of years for a redwood to become fully grown. They can live for up to 2,000 years.

Although the redwood is the tallest, some trees can be wider. The widest tree in the world is thought to be a cypress tree in Mexico. Its trunk is more than 11 m (36 feet) wide.

Out in the Open

Trees that live on the grasslands of Africa have to be tough, because there is so little rain. They have special ways of holding onto water.

Acacia

The tough acacia tree has long roots that seek out water deep underground. Its long, sharp thorns protect the tree from being eaten by browsing animals.

Giraffe

Sociable weaver bird

Acacia thorn

Trees are important for wildlife. Elephants and giraffes eat their leaves. They also provide shelter from the burning sun.

Baobab

The baobab tree has an enormous trunk. It uses the trunk to store water. The baobab's thick bark does not burn easily, which helps protect it from fires.

Fantastic Fruit

After the blossoms fall away, flowering trees will start to grow fruits. A fruit is the part of the tree that contains its **seeds**.

Early in summer, tiny fruits begin to appear on apple trees. They grow bigger and bigger throughout the warm summer months.

Badger

Fieldfare

Fruit attracts wildlife. Birds like to peck at fallen apples. Fruit also makes a tasty meal for badgers and mice.

Core

Seeds

By the end of the summer, the apples are ripe. If they are not picked by people, they fall from the tree onto the ground below.

Codling caterpillar

The caterpillars of codling moths make a tiny hole in some apples and eat their way to the middle. The middle of the apple is called the core. Apple seeds are in the core.

Taking Root

The roots are the parts of the tree that are usually underground. They are the first part of the tree to grow. Trees depend on their roots to live.

The roots of a tree spread very wide. Some are often just under the surface. Sometimes, you can see roots that have broken through the ground.

Surface root

The first root, called the taproot, grows straight down under the tree. This helps to hold the tree firmly to the ground. Other roots grow in different directions.

Taproot

Some trees have roots that grow deep into the ground, while others have shallow roots. Most conifers have very shallow roots.

The tips of the roots take in water and **nutrients** from the soil. The water travels through the roots to the rest of the tree.

Plant a Seed

Even the tallest tree was once just a small seed. Plant sunflower, pea, or bean seeds, and watch them grow. You'll also need a glass jar, some paper towels, water, and time!

1

Pour a little water into a glass jar, and swill it around so the sides get wet. Push paper towels inside the jar.

2

Sprinkle a little water onto the seeds, and place them between the paper and the side of the jar. The damp paper should hold the seeds in place.

Bean seed

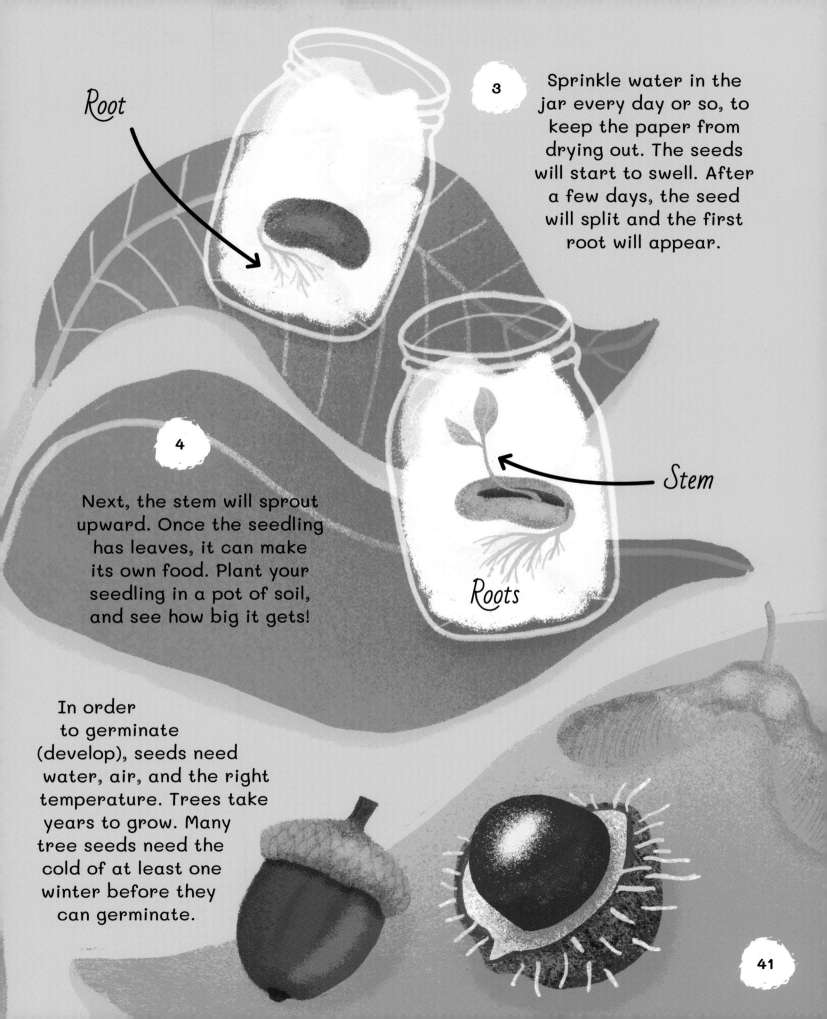

Root

3 Sprinkle water in the jar every day or so, to keep the paper from drying out. The seeds will start to swell. After a few days, the seed will split and the first root will appear.

Stem

4 Next, the stem will sprout upward. Once the seedling has leaves, it can make its own food. Plant your seedling in a pot of soil, and see how big it gets!

Roots

In order to germinate (develop), seeds need water, air, and the right temperature. Trees take years to grow. Many tree seeds need the cold of at least one winter before they can germinate.

Tropical Trees

Palm trees are able to live in places that are very warm. They grow in **rain forests**, deserts, and on the edges of **tropical** beaches.

Palms do not have branches. Instead, they have lots of large leaves that grow out of the top of the tree.

The tough, leathery leaves are known as "fronds." They are pointed at the tips, so that water falls off them easily in a tropical rainstorm.

A palm tree trunk is tall and fairly straight, and about the same thickness all the way up. The trunk is able to bend in tropical winds and storms.

The roots of palm trees stretch deep underground to find water. They do not grow as thick as other types of tree roots.

Trees in Danger

One-third of the land on Earth is covered with forests, but this is changing. People cut down trees to make space for farmland and new towns. This harms the **environment**.

In a natural forest, hundreds of different types of trees and plants grow. The animals that live there depend on this variety of plant life. This is called **biodiversity**.

When forests are cleared, many trees and plants die. The animals that lived there lose their homes.

Farms often grow just a few different types of plants, which means that fewer animals can live there.

44

People also make lots of waste called **pollution**, which can harm trees, plants, and animals.

Sometimes, fires start in forests. They can start by themselves in hot, dry weather. They can also be started by people. Forest fires can destroy hundreds of trees.

How to Help

Trees help our planet to be healthy. They clean our air and provide homes for many different types of animals. Find out how you can help protect our precious trees.

Try to use less paper. Make sure you write or draw on both sides of a sheet of paper, and use handkerchiefs, rather than tissues. These are great ways to use less.

When you really cannot use card and paper again, put it in the recycling box. This means that your waste paper is processed, so that it can be used to make new things.

Help create a clean living **environment** for trees by picking up litter whenever you can. Not only does litter look unpleasant, it can also pollute the soil and water needed for trees to grow.

Planting a tree is a great way to do something good for the environment. Many organizations hold tree-planting days. If you have outdoor space, you could plant your own tree.

GLOSSARY

Biodiversity   The variety of plants and animals found in a particular area.

Broadleaf   A type of deciduous tree with a bushy shape and wide, flat leaves.

Carbon dioxide   A gas found in the air. Plants take in carbon dioxide, and animals breathe it out.

Coniferous   Mostly evergreen trees that produce cones.

Deciduous   Trees that lose their leaves in winter.

Environment   The surroundings of an area, including living things and nonliving things.

Evergreen   Trees that keep their leaves throughout the year.

Germination   When a seed sprouts and starts to develop into a plant.

Glucose   A type of sugar.

Habitat   The natural home of an animal or plant.

Nectar   A sweet liquid produced by flowers that animals like to eat.

Nutrients   Substances that are important for the growth and development of plants and animals.

Oxygen   A natural gas found in the air that is necessary for all animal life on Earth.

Photosynthesis   The process by which plants and trees make their own food using sunlight, water, and carbon dioxide

Pollen   A sticky powder that plants produce as part of the process of making more plants.

Pollution   Harmful waste, including waste and chemicals, that dirties the air, land, or sea.

Rain forest   A thick forest found in warm, wet areas of the world.

Seed   The part of a plant that grows into a new plant.

Tropical   Characteristic of an area of the world that is warm or hot all year round.